3.36

D0919882

About the Book

Did you ever see small silver fish dancing on their tails in the sand? Grunion do this when they come out of the water to lay their eggs high on a sandy beach.

Grunion hunting is an exciting experience. All you need is your bare hands and a bag. In fact, that's all the law allows you to use! In her first book for Harvey House, Ann Stepp tells about the sport of grunion fishing and of the uncanny ability of this strange fish to predict the highest wave of the highest tide on which to ride ashore. Then, step-by-step, she shows the development of the eggs which they bury ashore beyond reach of the waves, and of the effects that tides and gravitation have upon this unique species.

GRUNION
Fish Out of Water

GRUNION

Fish Out of Water

ANN STEPP

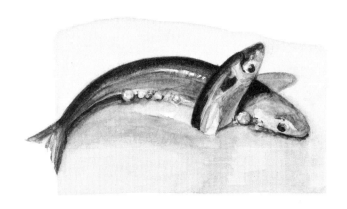

Illustrations by

Anne Lewis

HARVEY HOUSE, INC.
Publishers
Irvington-on-Hudson, N.Y.

For Doadie and Harry Terwilliger

J597

CONTENTS

A GRUNION RUN

Late on a starlighted spring evening, a barefoot teen-ager wearing cut-off blue jeans and carry-
ing an old pillow case ran in and out of the breaking
waves along a southern California beach. An
elderly white-haired man with a flashlight in one
hand and a gunnysack in the other sauntered not
far behind, waving his light back and forth along
the water's edge. Farther back, a family group hast-
ily gulped hot dogs they had roasted over an open
fire. All up and down the beach, people were wait-

ing. Many of them were barefoot. Most of them
carried flashlights, and all of them had a container
of one sort or another.

"Here they come!" someone shouted as a wave
rolled in and deposited dozens of shiny little fish
upon the sand. The teen-ager began to fill his pillow
case with them. The next wave deposited another
batch of several dozen and each succeeding wave
brought in hundreds more. The elderly man grab-

bed at one when an
unexpected wave soaked
his clothing and washed the
fish from his reach. Children and
grown-ups alike laughed at each other's
attempts to grab the slippery squirming fish. This
was a grunion run, and grunion, according to California law, can be caught only with bare hands.

Soon the teen-ager's pillow case bulged with
the silver fish. He counted with pride his catch of
over 200. The exercise was invigorating to the old

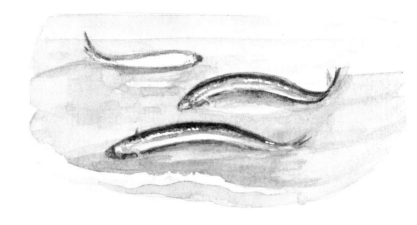

man. For some, the roar of the waves and the sport of chasing after the dancing, slippery fish was entertainment enough. For others, such as the family group, grunion provided a fish-fry for dinner. They have a delicate flavor, especially when rolled in a mixture of flour, cornmeal and salt and then pan-fried.

The grunion is a slender fish with a bluish-green back and bright silvery sides. It lives mainly along the sandy beaches of southern California from near Morro Bay southward for approximately two-thirds the length of Baja California on the Pacific Coast side. No one knows why it has so limited a habitat. It is one of the mysteries of the grunion. Nor is it understood why the California grunion prefer for its spawning certain beaches such as Long Beach, Belmont Shore, Huntington Beach, Corona

SPAWNING AREAS OF THE GRUNION

del Mar, Cabrillo Beach and La Jolla, when it has the choice of the entire California coast and part of Mexico. There are beaches similar to these which the grunion ignore.

Once it was thought that the grunion must have a homing instinct, explaining why they chose the same particular beaches year after year. In 1927, a new artificial beach was built at the base of the breakwater in Los Angeles Harbor. The grunion made a run on this beach that year and have continued to do so each year since.

Grunion come out of the water to lay their eggs high on the moist, sandy beaches. This in itself makes them unusual. What makes them scientifically unique, however, is their uncanny ability to know precisely *when* to come ashore.

A grunion run may last from one to three hours. The peak of the run occurs between thirty minutes and an hour after the first fish come in. The number of fish on the beach varies from none to thousands. Although grunion runs are made on many beaches, they are often concentrated on a short stretch of each beach. People miss good runs sometimes because they become discouraged and go home if the fish do not appear within half an hour after high tide. Were they to wait fifteen minutes longer, they would see the beach so covered with the silver fish that they could not walk without stepping on them.

Grunion have a tide time-table instinct. They spawn by the tidal waves with a fixed regularity that is unexcelled by man. From February through August, when the tides rise the highest, grunion swim out of the sea. Their instinct tells them when

the water has risen to its highest peak of a particular tide.

They never make their run to shore until after the peak tide when the tides have begun to fall. The spawning run of the females is forerun by a few lone male grunion, called scouts, who make sure conditions are correct. Grunion will not run in a rocky area. Nor can they spawn on sand that is too hard, because the eggs would lay on top of the sand rather than beneath it and would be eaten by birds or dried by the sun. Often they avoid areas that are overcrowded. If the male scouts are picked up by people on the beach, the chances are lessened that the grunion will run that night because the females await the return of the scouts to lead them onto the beach. When the tide drops a foot or more from its peak, the run stops as suddenly as it started. The fish disappear as if they had been signalled. Once the run stops, the grunion will not appear again that night.

Actually there are only four nights at each high tide when the female grunion can lay her eggs

successfully. This was confirmed as long ago as 1918 by the late Dr. William F. Thompson of the California State Fisheries Laboratories, whose studies indicated that grunion appear on the first four nights following the highest tides of the month. The best runs usually occur on the second and third nights of the four.

The heaviest runs occur in April, May and June. The grunion hunter, who must obtain a state fishing license if he is over sixteen, is not allowed to hunt grunion in April and May. Nor is he permitted to dig pits in the sand to trap them. These regulations help to insure the survival of the species. June and July runs are usually good, while August runs are generally lighter.

Most visitors to California have never heard of grunion fishing. Moreover, there are native Californians who have never gone grunion fishing for fear grunion do not really exist, and that they might be victims of a practical joke. After all, when one is invited to go fishing at midnight with only a gunny sack for equipment, one can hardly be blamed for skepticism.

SPAWNING

Why grunion come ashore to lay their eggs is a scientific mystery. The timing involved in the entire spawning and egg development process is difficult to equal in nature. Although the spawning behavior of grunion can easily be observed, most grunion hunters never see it because they are too eager to catch the fish. The female, her abdomen swollen with ripe eggs, swims onto the beach. She is accompanied by at least two males — sometimes by as many as eight.

The female swims as far ashore as she can. Then she begins to dig herself into the moist sand by arching her body with her head up and vigorously wriggling her tail back and forth. The stirring of the sand makes it soft and fluid and the female actually drills herself downward until she is buried up to her pectoral fins. After she has buried herself, the males, lying on top of the sand, curve around the female's body and emit a fluid called *milt*. At this time, the female twists and bends from side to side, emitting her eggs two or three inches beneath the surface in a pocket of the sand. The males immediately start to wriggle toward the water.

The milt flows down about the body of the female until it reaches the eggs, which become fer-

Returning to the sea

tilized upon contact with it. The female then frees herself from the sand and returns to the sea with the next wave.

This ceremonial-like procedure takes only about thirty seconds. It happens so quickly that on-lookers hardly realize what has occurred. Some grunion spawn so rapidly that they make a round trip with the same wave. An occasional fish sometimes misses a wave and flops on the sand until the next wave. It can survive on the beach for several minutes.

After the spawning, the tide remains low enough so that the surf does not reach the eggs until two weeks later when the next high tides occur. The eggs are kept warm by the covering sands. The grunion nursery is safe from birds and the drying sun. The two-week interval between high tides is exactly right for the incubation of the eggs.

If the eggs are not dug out by the first series of high tides that follow, they will remain healthy for another two weeks. Then the next series of high tides can release them and carry them out to sea. If the second series misses the eggs, they will not survive.

The very existence of the grunion is linked with the tidal waves. For example, if the eggs are buried anywhere but far above the average high tides, the eggs will be freed long before they are developed. If the eggs are buried too far above the water and the waves cannot reach them, they will not hatch. Nor will they hatch if they are not uncovered and agitated by the waves of the sea.

Another species of fish, the Gulf grunion, is known to have habits similar to the California grunion. The Gulf grunion are found in the upper part of the Gulf of California and make their runs earlier in the season than the California grunion. No other known fish in the world leave the water to spawn.

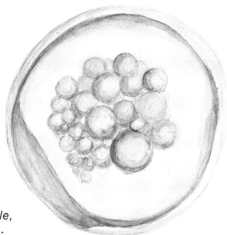

*One hour after fertilization,
the embryonic disc is visible,
but there is no cell division.*

DEVELOPMENT OF THE EGG

After a dramatic run of grunion has disappeared into the sea, there is nothing on the surface of the beach to indicate that thousands of eggs are lying in a nursery beneath the sand. They lay three to six inches below the surface in clusters that are about the size of ping pong balls. Each cluster contains approximately 2,000 eggs.

Even though the eggs are deposited by the female at a depth of two inches, they get a thicker sand coverlet as subsequent waves wash more sand

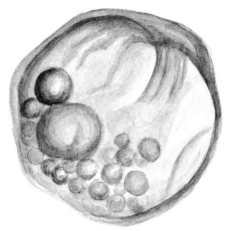

At 36 hours, the outline of the embryonic fish can be seen. Bulges at the head end will become eyes.

upon the beach. There is a split second when each wave loses its momentum and stops. It is at this moment that it drops sand which provides further protection for the grunion nursery.

The sand remains moist during the first few days following high tides. After ten days, the surface becomes completely dried. In fact, the surface of the sand may be so hot that barefoot surfers and sun-bathers must walk fast to keep from burning their feet. The temperature of the sand two inches below the surface, however, is only slightly warmed, permitting the eggs to retain sufficient moisture to remain healthy.

The magic unfolding of life through cell division takes place in each tiny grunion egg during a two-week period. A low-power magnifier would show the tiny bright orange eggs to be the size of a grain of sand when they are laid.

Grunion eggs are a favorite food of sandpipers, birds which run up and down the beach during low tide poking their beaks into the sand looking for food. A group of sandpipers huddled together on the beach usually indicates that they have discovered the grunion nursery and are having their lunch.

In a fertilized grunion egg, cloudiness represents the multiplying of cells and can be seen during the first three days after spawning. The newly deposited egg contains many dark orange oil globules which vary in size and number. Development con-

Sandpipers

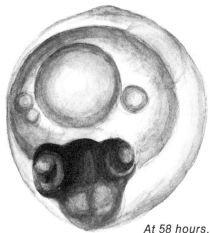

At 58 hours, the round pupils of the eyes are visible.

tinues until only one large uncolored oil globule remains in the yolk sac of the young fish.

The first recognizable features of the fish embryo are its head and large eyes. At two-and-a-half or three days, the eyes and brain cleavage begin to develop.

The first spasm of heart tissue occurs at three days. The heart beat is irregular at first, but soon develops into a small pump with regular beats. By the end of four days, a separate heart chamber with definite valve action develops, producing movement of blood corpuscles.

After five days, the blood circulation moves to and from the tail. Corpuscles move into all cell tis-

EARLY STAGES OF THE GRUNION

*Egg of grunion
before fertilization.
Diameter 1.55/1.65 mm.*

*Same egg
immediately
after fertilization*

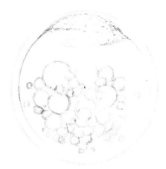

*12 hours after
fertilization*

*34 hours after
fertilization*

*60 hours after
fertilization*

*132 hours after
fertilization*

Larva of two week-old grunion — 3 mm. long

25

sues. After another half day, the circulation is complete and visible. The grunion's ribs, backbone, fins, and tail are now identifiable. At the end of eight days, a dark color develops and its eyes move.

Some of the eggs, but not many, are capable of hatching after eight and a half days. Most of the eggs will hatch at ten-and-a-half days under right conditions, and the fish will continue to develop as they swim. The ideal incubation time is fourteen days.

When the high tide comes again, the water erodes the beach and the buried eggs are set free. The two weeks have given the baby fish time to develop. The salt water immediately triggers the hatching, and the baby grunion swim into the sea. They return to shore only when they are full grown and ready to spawn. Most of the grunion's life is spent within one to three miles offshore, where they stay in water 15 to 40 feet deep. This phase of their life history is not well known. It is believed that they never stray far from the beach in which they spawn.

For purposes of laboratory studies, grunion eggs have been dug out on the very night that they were laid, then kept in moist sand in glass jars for observation. The newly-laid eggs are like tiny orange balls that gradually lose their color after the

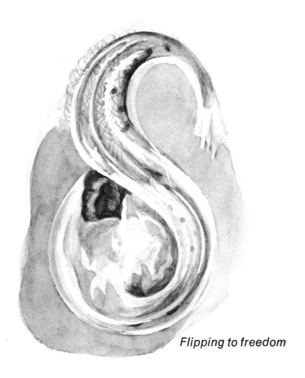

Flipping to freedom

heartbeat of the baby fish develops. Those that remain orange after four days are eggs which the milt of the male did not reach to fertilize. Those that turn white are fertilized eggs that become damaged before they mature. Eggs that will hatch into grunion take on a transparent appearance.

Salt water (sea water) was placed in some of the laboratory jars after ten to twelve days, and the jars were shaken vigorously to simulate the action of an ocean wave. Almost immediately, the eggs hatched with baby grunion popping out and swimming about. The same experiment failed when tried with fresh water.

Low Tide

THE CHANGING OCEAN

The survival of the grunion depends upon their ability to predict the ever-changing ocean. To appreciate the spectacular timing of their egg-laying, we must understand tides.

People living near an ocean might see rock formations for a certain portion of the day. A few hours later, the rocks have disappeared. Although they have not moved, the rocks have been covered over by a rise of the water. The changes in the water levels of the ocean are called tides.

High Tide

Because of these continual changes, the grunion's timing must be perfect. As the tide rises, sand washes out to sea. But when the tide reaches its peak and starts to fall, sand is returned and deposited upon the beach. If grunion were to spawn on the rising high tides, their eggs would be washed out to sea with the sand. During the ten days that are needed for a baby grunion to develop, the egg must be untouched by sea water.

Centuries ago men wondered about the changing tides and tried to explain them. Some thought that ghosts and witches were especially active during certain phases of the moon. Superstitious people thought that a full moon had the power to drive men mad. Fantastic stories were told to explain the rise and fall of the shoreline. According to one story, a god lived at the bottom of the sea. When the god gulped in a mouthful of water, he caused a low tide. When he spat out the water, there was a high tide. Others accepted the explanation that the tides occurred simply because the ocean sloshed back and forth as the earth rotated on its axis, comparing it to the sloshing back and forth of coffee in a cup as it is carried across a room.

For many years men suspected that the moon affected the earth and the sea. In 1687, Sir Isaac Newton gave the correct explanation that everything in the universe exerts a pull on everything else. Even a small object exerts some force. The moon, as well as the sun and all other heavenly bodies exert a pull on the earth.

The strength of the pull on the earth by another body depends upon the mass and distance of the object from the earth. Of all the billions of planets and stars in our universe, only the moon

GRUNION SPAWNING CHART

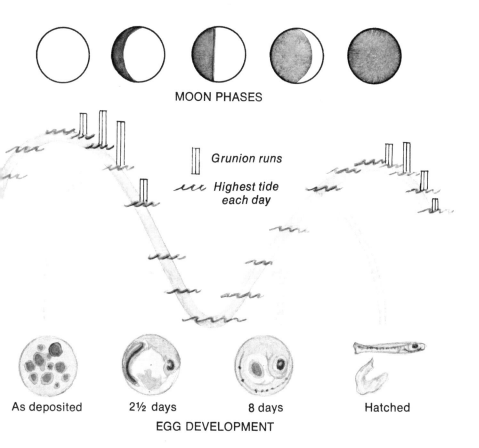

MOON PHASES

Grunion runs

Highest tide
each day

As deposited   2½ days   8 days   Hatched

EGG DEVELOPMENT

and sun are close enough to the earth to cause tides.

The distance between earth and the moon is
approximately 240,000 miles, while the distance between earth and the sun is nearly 93,000,000 miles.
The sun's mass is millions of times greater than the

MOON, SUN AND TIDES

New Moon

First Quarter

Full
Moon

Last Quarter

moon's. Since the moon is so much closer to earth, however, its pull has a greater effect on the tides of earth.

The moon and sun are like two magnets pulling at the earth. It is this force which makes the ocean tides go higher at certain times. This force is called gravity. The water on the earth is drawn slightly toward these two bodies. It is this small movement of the sea which causes tidal actions.

As the moon travels around the earth, it is not always an equal distance away. When it is closest to the earth, its pull is strongest and tides are twenty to forty per cent higher than when it is farthest from the earth.

CAUSES OF THE TIDES

Nature has always provided the grunion with the knowledge of the tides. Man can now calculate tides all over the world using machinery, computers and other tools. The grunion needs no machine to do its calculating.

Since solid earth does not stretch noticeably, the pull of the moon is not visible. The movement of solid earth is about 4½ inches, and can be detected only by delicate instruments. We do not feel or see these "land tides." Water, however, is free to move and pile up. We are aware of ocean tides bcause they rise and fall many feet rather than a few inches. From minute to minute, the level of the ocean changes. When the tide is low, the ocean becomes deeper. When the tide is high, the water is spread out and the ocean becomes more shallow.

The ocean does not rise and fall only against land, but also in mid-ocean, where it is not noticed. People aboard a ship can neither see nor feel the waters' rise and fall because the ship rises and falls with it. The tide movement is apparent only when there is something against which to measure the change, such as land or a pile of rocks.

The moon also affects the atmosphere. Rises and falls take place daily. Because we live at the bottom of the air rather than at the top, we are totally unaware of its tidal movements.

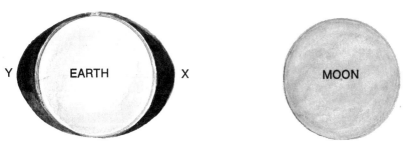

The ocean at X is nearer the moon than the solid part of the earth and gets a stronger pull.

This makes the water bulge away from the earth, and high tides occur. Because the solid part is closer to the moon than the ocean at Y, it is pulled away from Y. This also makes a bulge at point Y and it is high tide, too.

The tidal bulges change locations as the moon orbits the earth. The spinning of the earth on its axis also causes different parts of the ocean to be in line with the moon at different times. This accounts for the changing of the tide levels.

When the sun is in line with earth and moon, the total pull on the oceans is even stronger. The extra-high tides happen twice a month during Full Moon and New Moon. This is when the grunion choose to come ashore.

From February through August, when the grunion spawn, the highest of the two daily high tides always occurs during the night. This is fortunate for the safety of the grunion. If they had to ride a high tide onto shore in the daytime, the shore birds might eat them.

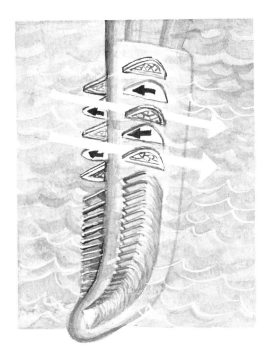

Gill of a fish *showing how water and blood flow between the gill plates in opposite directions. Oxygen from the water flowing over the gills is absorbed into the blood.*

BLOOD

WATER

GROWTH OF GRUNION

Grunion, like all fish, are cold-blooded. This means that their body temperature is the same as the water in which they live.

Most fish cannot take oxygen from the air as animals do. They open and close their mouths to take in water. The water goes into the fish's mouth, passes over its gills and flows out the gill flaps. As the water passes the gills, the blood in the gills absorbs oxygen from the water. The gills do for the grunion what our lungs do for us.

Baby grunion grow rapidly. Within ten minutes after hatching, they double in size. Their rapid growth continues during the summer, but slows down in the winter. By the end of the next spring they have grown to about five inches in length.

The grunion are ready for their first spawning a year after hatching in early summer. A one year-old grunion lays about 1,000 eggs each time she spawns. A two year-old or a three year-old will lay from 2,000 to 3,000 eggs, although the number varies with the size of the fish.

Only the older females spawn during the early part of the season. Gradually, the fish born the previous year come onto the beach. During April and May, fish of all ages spawn. After this time, the number is less.

Some species of fish die after spawning — but not the grunion. It remains near its chosen breeding grounds until time to go ashore again. Grunion spawn four to eight times a year. The normal length of life for a grunion is two or three years. Occasionally one lives four years.

An adult grunion body is covered by a protective coating of scales which overlap each other like the shingles on a roof. A thin, tight-fitting layer

of skin outside these scales contains glands that se-
crete a slime all over the fish. The slimy secretion
helps to prevent parasites and diseased organisms
from growing on the fish. It is most noticeable when
you try to catch the grunion with your hands and it
wriggles and slips free of your grasp.

The fish's scale consists of a material similar to our fingernails. Deeper in the skin there is a larger area of each scale covered or overlapped by the scale behind it. The scale continues to grow throughout the fish's life, pushing outward and enlarging as the fish grows bigger. Thus the total number of scales on a grunion's body remains the same throughout its life. New scales replace those that are accidentally lost.

Fish scientists can tell much about a fish's past life by examining its scales. "Growing rings" appear on each scale as it increases in size. A heavy line on the scale appears where there is no growth and when growth starts again.

During the spawning months from February to August, growth stops. The fish grow only during the fall and winter. The cessation of growth causes a mark to form on each scale. Thus, by counting marks, the age of a fish can be determined. The average full-grown grunion is between five to seven inches in length. Female grunion are larger than males of the same age. Males are seldom more than six inches.

Grunion feed on plankton, the tiny plants and animals that swim and float in the surface water.

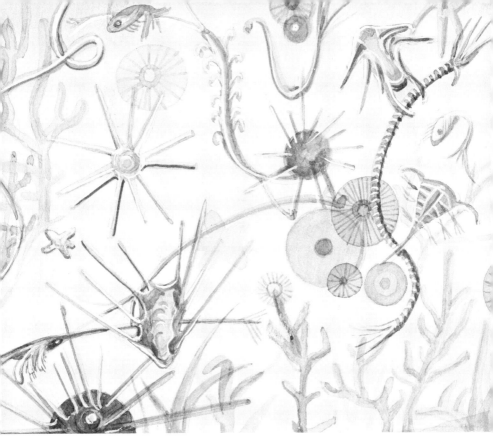

Plankton

The plant particles of plankton are called *diatoms*.
The animal particles of plankton are called *cope-
pods*.

Young grunion have been kept in laboratories
for observation by scientists, but it has not proved
successful. The young grunion die after about a
month. Something — probably the necessary plankton — is lacking in the laboratory's salt water tanks.
Because of this, scientists have been unable to ob-
serve the growth of grunion for more than six weeks.

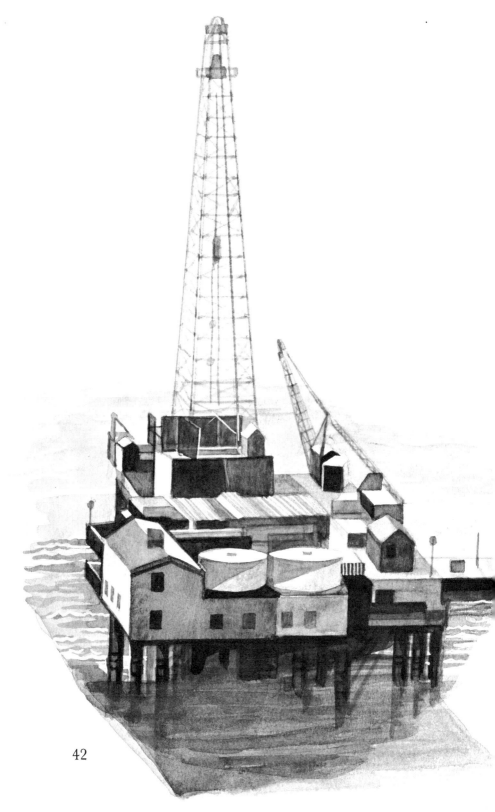

GRUNION HISTORY AND FUTURE

Although grunion do not exist in great numbers, there seems to be no danger of their depletion, despite the popularity of grunion fishing.

In 1926, when the grunion runs became noticeably smaller, a closed season on grunion fishing was enforced during the months of April, May and June. By 1948, the grunion population was large enough to allow a longer open season for the fishermen, so June was added to the list of open months.

Grunion have never been sufficiently abundant to support a commercial fishery. Even so, their runs remain plentiful despite the hazards they encounter — eager fishermen, and the pollution of beaches.

On January 28, 1969, oil gushed from a fissure in the ocean floor beneath a Union Oil Company drilling rig $5\frac{1}{2}$ miles off Santa Barbara, spreading a carpet of crude petroleum along thirty miles of the southern California coast. A clean-up effort restored the beaches, but many sea animals and birds died. The worst damage, however, came from the action of the chemical used to dissolve the oil. Fortunately it was a low-gravity crude oil that flowed upon the surface of the water. It seemed to have little effect upon marine organisms or fish, including grunion, whose runs in the Santa Barbara area are sparse. The clean-up activities along the beaches, however, certainly would have disturbed eggs deposited in the sand.

According to the California State Fisheries Laboratory, grunion have not migrated out of the Santa Barbara area as a result of the oil slick. Several experiments have been made with grunion eggs to determine whether the oil would inhibit their hatching. According to all tests, the eggs hatched.

In the early 1960's, the Space and Information System Division of North American Aviation Company was commissioned by the federal government to do research of Life Support Systems for the moon landing. One aspect of their studies of the gravitational effects on living things was an attempt to determine if the grunion could measure gravitational force. It was suspected that this might be the key to the grunion's ability to predict the highest part of the tides.

As part of the experiment, a magnetic field seven times greater than that of the earth was introduced into the tide water of Cabrillo Beach to determine its effect upon the grunion's timing.

Their conclusions indicated that the increased magnetic field did not seem to affect grunion and that their runs continued as usual.

What, then, is the secret of the grunion and its internal clock? It remains one of the unsolved mysteries of the ocean, puzzling biologists and scientists, who continue to be astonished at the ability of grunion to present themselves on the beach at precisely the right time for the greatest possible survival of their young.

The grunion is indeed a unique fish.

About the Author

If you should see an attractive redhead digging in the sand at daybreak at Huntington Beach, California, it might be Ann Stepp hunting for grunion eggs so that the students in her science classes can watch them hatch. A teacher at Lampson Junior High School at Garden Grove, California, Miss Stepp earned a Bachelor of Science degree from the University of Oklahoma and a Master of Arts degree from Chapman College. She is a member of the National Science Teachers Association.

About the Artist

A native of Boston, Anne Lewis studied at the Boston Museum of Fine Arts and was graduated from the Massachusetts School of Art, now known as the Massachusetts College of Art. Now a resident of New York City, Mrs. Lewis has designed and illustrated many children's books. Among them are *The Story of Light, Shakespeare for Young Players, The Story of Birds of North America, Let's Learn About the Orchestra,* and *Toss and Catch,* which she wrote as well as illustrated.